Blooming flowers

Short Stories for Little Buds

"You are beautiful
You are unique
That is it
That you have to believe.."

Shaheera

Made with ♥ on the Notion Press Platform
www.notionpress.com

About Blooming Flowers..

Where flowers bloom, so does hope. A flower is all about beautiful vibrant colours spreading so much of positivity. They give you a sense of calmness when you are around them and the buds growing possess the same quality.

Blooming Flowers associates those growing children as little buds which grow with time into beautiful Blooming flowers and spreading their tranquility. They deserve the best of nourishment to spread and give the best to this world.

The values instilled in one's childhood has a great influence in his adulthood which help him overcome all the obstacles and become very successful in life.

This book contains short stories for those beautiful buds who are sure to spread their positive radiance and are slowly growing into beautiful "Blooming Flowers."

Context

1.Believe in yourself.

A poor man named Shankar earned his living by selling balloons. His daughter Ria's school fees had to be paid. Her father worked very hard but still all the expenses of the house were met with difficulty. So the coming week she decided to help her father increase his sales.

Ria felt very bad about being poor. All her classmates were from well to do families. Her friends came to school by luxurious cars whereas she had to walk to school from her home. She would borrow books, uniforms and shoes from her seniors who had passed the class to help her her parents cope up with the expense of her education. Her classmates had unique stationary items but she tried her best to make use of the pencil till it was difficult to hold it between her fingers. She avoided making friends because maintaining the level of status they had was a dream for her…

Inspite of the hustle and bustle on the street, Ria and her father were going unnoticed by the children passing by. In order to cheer her up Shankar released a pink balloon which caught the attention of the children eating ice cream at the ice cream stall. Children got attracted and it helped Ria increase her sales.

There was this cute little boy who had his eyes struck on the balloons. He went towards the balloons and pulled Shankar's shirt gesturing him to listen to what this boy had to say. Out of curiosity he asked, "Uncle does the black balloon also fly?"

Shankar was moved by the little boy's question and stroke his hair with love. He replied to him and said, "Oh yes Son, see" and went the black balloon in the air. "It is what is inside that makes it go up and not the colour that influences the balloon to go up."

Ria was astounded by what her father said to the little boy. Her being poor made her feel sad many times. She faced a lot of difficulties in life. She promised herself to work very hard in school and go high up like the balloon. Her being poor did not matter like the colour of the balloon. So what if she was poor. She thought, what matters is my attitude. She was very worried that her father would get her married due to the insufficiency of finance in the house. She too wanted to be educated and fulfil all her desires. Her will to work hard and her positive attitude made her successful in studies. She scored very good marks. Impressed with her performance in the class the school management offered her a scholarship each year. Years passed by and a balloon seller's daughter started her own balloon venture. Financial crisis were long forgotten. Ria too had a beautiful house and a luxurious car. All the needs of the house were easily met. She had friends whom she could enjoy with. Festivals seemed more joyous to her.

Her inner positive attitude made her go high up like the air inside the colourful balloon. She wished so much when she was a child and with hard work she now had everything she had wished for. It is never to bad to have so many desires but what's important is that we try to fulfil them with the right means in the right manner with the right attitude..

2.Never to boast

There was once a very boastful boy. His name was Ramesh. He was too good at studies. Topper of the class you see. He did not respect the other students of the class. The students who scored below average marks had to be insulted by him very often.

One day Ramesh said to another boy named Aakash, “Look how intelligent I am. I can solve all the sums you give me. Maths is on my tips.” He laughed to no limit looking at his English exam paper. Made fun of him ridiculously.

Aakash got very embarrased and further started to cry when he saw boys and girls laughing at Ramesh's comment.

Aakash tried many times to get successful in studies but he failed each time. Academics just wasn't his cup of tea.

All the students were passing out from school that year. It was the last day of school when all students were making promises to be there for each other whenever in need.

After five years students planned a reunion. Everybody was excited. They had all grown up in these five years. One was about to become a doctor, one of them a botanist, engineer and some of them were working in good multinational companies.

One of the boys had arrived by a very luxurious car. All the other students looked at the car admiringly. It was a very expensive car. When he stepped out all the other students were left admiring.

“Aakash,” everyone looked surprised. “What are you upto now a days? “Tejaswi asked,” How are you?” Everybody got curious while some got jealous.

Aakash feeling content said, “Thank you so much dear friends for all the love. I am an artist now. Ever since I was a child, I loved painting. Never knew when my hobby would become my profession.”

Ramesh stood leaning at the back table and did not have the courage to meet Aakash’s eyes. How often he had made fun of him. Ramesh inspite of topping the class everytime failed to get a good job. All his efforts were in vain.

How successful he had been once upon a time. He realised his mistake. Success along with hard work needs good morals. They go side by side. We should never look down upon someone who maybe less than us in some field. He may be best in the other.

3.Help others and help yourself.

It was a rainy season. Rosy's mother had bought her a beautiful umbrella. One day when Rosy was about to leave from school it started to rain. Rosy took out her brand new umbrella happily.

Dolly, who was Rosy's classmate had no umbrella so she was totally wet. Dolly asked Rosy, "Can you share your umbrella with me." Rosy snapped, "No, my mother just gifted it to me yesterday, its my brand new umbrella."

Dolly was helpless now, so she decided to go home without an umbrella. Rosy was walking home happily and not before too long she fell in a puddle. She hurt her elbow and knee and it was bleeding.

Dolly who had been walking along saw her cry. She rushed to help her. She assured Rosy to not to worry and thought of ways to help her. “Oh, don’t cry Rosy, I am here for you.” Dolly said.

At this moment Dolly pulled out a long scarf around her neck. She tore it into two halves. She tied one part of it on her bleeding knee and the other half on the bleeding elbow. She helped her stand and walk home.

Dolly's scarf was too gifted by her mother. It was a handmade scarf. Not once did Dolly give a thought and reached out for help. Generous Dolly helped helped Rosy. Rosy was ashamed and apologised for her behaviour. Since then they both became friends and always helped each other.

Forgiveness can generate unexpected power. A wise man always turns his enemies into friends. A narrow minded person will turn his friends into enemies.

4.Self contentment

Abaan and Hussain were neighbours who became good friends gradually. Abaan had been a labourer once upon a time and with wages earned he would incur his household expenses and used to save two percent of his income.

He worked so hard that in years he had started his own retail venture of kid's toys. His always being content brought him success and lead him to good sleeps at night.

Hussain on the other hand was never satisfied. He always wanted to become more rich. He stressed himself so much that it detoriated his mental health and physical health. He had a big farm and he earned a lot by selling his crops nationwide. With the want of doing a bigger business internationally he sold of his farm to Abaan and started a new venture in U.S.A.

Abaan was way too happy to have bought a farm as well. While watering the plants he saw a beautiful sparkling stone lying next to the plant. He found it so beautiful that he decorated it on the showcase shelf in his living area.

One day Abaan's old friend had come to pay him a visit. His eyes fell on the shinig stone. He said, "Abaan it seems precious, why dont you get it examined." He took the suggestion seriously and got it examined by a jeweller. The jeweller was startled after examining.

He screamed. "It's a diamond." Abaan was way to happy to know this and when he went to his farm, he saw his farm was filled with similar stones. He couldn't believe his eyes. He danced and jumped with joy.

Overnight he had become even more rich. Abaan's contentment would lead him to be so rich, he never thought. The grass is always greener on the other side. We should always be happy and content with what we have.

He sold off the diamonds and from the money he earned he bought a land and started his own property business.

5.You are Unique

Once Tina thought to herself, “I dont like me, I need to change. Wish I was like Priya. The way she talks, walks is all so awesome. She is very smart. I have taken French because she has also taken that subject. She takes smart decisions.”

Tina

But Priya was all influenced by Radhika. Her dressing style was just beginning to be like Radhika's. Her behaviour patterns were too becoming like her. Priya didn't know the A,b,c of volleyball but Radhika opted for it and so she opted for it too.

Priya

But Radhika was all influenced by Ananya. Ananya wore nothing less than Armaani. Radhika couldn't afford it but she somehow finds means of convincing her parents to shop from the most expensive mall. So Tina is all influenced by Priya. Priya is all influenced by Radhika. Radhika is all influenced by Ananya and Ananya is all influenced by???

TINA.

Ananya is all influenced by Tina. She loves Tina's soft hearted nature. She wants to be just like Tina. Amazingly all of us are unique. We should just follow our heart and know our selves well. There is nothing that can stop us from being appreciated and loved by everyone. We are all special in different unique ways.

Being just you makes it easy for people to know and understand you. This results in helping us getting the right kind of friends which lasts for a lifetime. We also take correct decissions about our life which helps us become successful.

www.ingramcontent.com/pod-product-compliance
Lightning Source LLC
LaVergne TN
LVHW021350160826
845679LV00008B/1562

* 9 7 9 8 8 9 4 1 5 2 0 7 3 *